Stephen Curry

The Inspiring Story of NBA Superstar Stephen Curry

Table of Contents

Introduction

Thank you for taking the time to pick up this book on Stephen Curry!

This book covers the topic of NBA superstar Stephen Curry, and aims to serve as a biography to date of his incredible life and career.

As you will soon discover, Steph Curry wasn't expected my many to even make it to the NBA. He was an undersized, unathletic point guard, who didn't appear to be NBA material. Despite all odds, he persevered and has gone on to change he game of basketball with his incredible shooting ability.

A multiple time NBA Champion, Stephen Curry has already achieved a lot in his short professional career. This book will discuss exactly what Curry's basketball career has involved so far, and what might be next for the young champion.

Once again, thanks for choosing this book, I hope you find it to be helpful!

Chapter 1: Steph as a Child

Wardell Stephen Curry's incredible basketball talent should not come as a surprise to anyone. His father is Dell Curry, a former NBA player popularly known for his three-point shooting ability.

Those who have known Dell since his NBA days expected that at least one of his children would follow in his footsteps. True enough, Steph is now part of the NBA.

But contrary to what most people initially thought, Steph is not living under the shadow of his dad. Dell had an incredible career in the NBA, but Steph has also successfully made a name for himself on his own.

Dell used to live a modest life in Grottoes, Virginia with his parents. They didn't have that much money to buy toys but his caring father, Wardell "Jack" Curry, was constantly thinking of activities for his children so they would not get bored at home.

One day, Jack decided to build a makeshift basketball hoop for Dell. It was basically a fiberglass board attached to a light pole. The hoop was so small that Dell had to get close to the basket to shoot the ball. Nonetheless, Dell liked his makeshift basketball hoop. He eventually started to take long jump shots on the smaller ring, which helped him perfect his jump shot.

Steph was born in Akron, Ohio on March 14, 1988 but, as a young child, he grew up constantly visiting his grandparents in Grottoes. At his grandparents' house, Steph would practice his jump shot on the very same ring his father had grown up with.

Growing up, Steph was exposed to different types of sports. During his childhood, their family also had to move from one place to another due to Dell's profession. Aside from Ohio, they also experienced living in Canada and North Carolina. Steph excelled at basketball and decided to seriously pursue playing at the collegiate level. This, of course, paved the way for him to make the NBA.

Steph's Sporty Parents

Dell grew up with an intense passion for basketball. In high school, his practice area would either be a barn or their yard and, in each practice, he would aim to reach five hundred shots.

He successfully displayed his basketball skills at Fort Defiance High School where he was recognized for being the highest-scoring player of his time. Such recognition allowed him to be featured in a high school basketball game hosted by McDonald's in 1982.

Aside from basketball, Dell also displayed his excellent baseball skills in high school. In fact, he was even drafted in the Major League Baseball twice – first, by the Texas Rangers and, second, by the Baltimore Orioles. He was passionate about baseball too but when he realized he could not play the sport during winter season, he opted to focus on basketball – a sport he could play any time of the year.

Dell chose to study at Virginia Tech University where he had the opportunity to play for the Hokies basketball team. Beginning 1983, he played with the team in the National

Invitational Tournament. There, he managed to exhibit his stellar basketball skills.

In 1984, the Hokies team did not emerge victorious in the Metropolitan Athletic Conference Tournament. However, Dell helped his team bag victories in the NIT Tournament. In the same year, the team joined the National Collegiate Athletic Association Tournament where he continued to display his exceptional skills. He impressed the National Basketball Association and was drafted by the Utah Jazz in 1986.

As an NBA rookie, Dell was not given much playing time by the Utah Jazz. He was then traded to the Cleveland Cavaliers where his playing time slightly increased. In 1988, he was traded to the Charlotte Hornets where his playing time improved as well as his statistics. For a decade, he played for Charlotte. During this time, Steph and his brother Seth were constantly seen at games watching their father play. This continued when Dell eventually played for the Milwaukee Bucks and the Toronto Raptors. It was in 2002 when Dell finally decided to retire.

Sonya Adams Curry, Steph's mom, was also known to be an athletic student from grade school to college. She excelled in three sports, namely, basketball, volleyball, and track and field. Like Dell, she also studied at Virginia Tech University where she earned a scholarship while playing for the university's volleyball team. Her outstanding skills allowed her to play in the All-Metropolitan League team.

Sonya and Dell met at Virginia Tech. In 1988, when Dell was playing for the Charlotte Hornets, they decided to get married.

Steph's Younger Years

Steph spent his early school years at the Christian Montessori School at Lake Norman, a school founded by his mother Sonya. According to the Curry family, the experiences of Steph and his siblings when attending that school are the reason behind them having such a closely-knit family.

Steph and his siblings grew up with a disciplinarian mom. There were many times when Steph would not be allowed to play because he skipped doing household chores.

Despite being athletes, Dell and Sonya did not promote sports in their household. The Curry children – Steph, Seth, and Sydel – were raised with a clear understanding that their priorities should be faith, family, school, and nothing else. It wasn't that they were not allowed to play any sport. They were, of course, allowed to play. However, Dell and Sonya didn't force any of their children to pursue a career in sports.

Growing up, Steph extremely enjoyed playing basketball with Seth. They would usually play the entire day in their backyard and would not stop until it got dark. It never entered their minds that, someday, they would both become professional basketball players.

Every time they visited Grottoes, the young Curry brothers never failed to play basketball using the makeshift hoop built by their grandfather, Jack. Just like his dad, Steph mastered making shots on the smaller ring. Aside from that, Steph learned to creatively dribble the ball on his grandfather's rocky and muddy yard which ultimately honed his ball-handling skills.

After the death of his grandfather Jack in 1991 due to a heart attack, Steph no longer visited Grottoes as often as he used to. Instead, he found himself regularly using the half court at their Charlotte residence. Having gotten used to the makeshift hoop in Grottoes, he noticed how easy it was to play on their NBA-quality court.

Steph's Exceptional Basketball Skills in School

The Currys were residing in Canada when Steph was in middle school. He was studying at Queensway Christian School and was playing for the Saints basketball team. During this time, he was already exhibiting exceptional basketball skills and even helped the Saints emerge victorious for two consecutive years. This was also the time when he started to grow more and more interested in taking basketball seriously.

In those days, Steph was constantly seen watching the Raptors games live, not just to watch his father, but to analyze each game. He was very observant of the plays, the players' moves, the referee's calls, and all the other details of each game. There was a time when a camera crew approached the then-teenager Steph where he expressed his dream of becoming an NBA player. However, in spite of him being a remarkable Saints player, his build was small and lanky. He didn't appear to have the size to one day make the NBA.

Nonetheless, the Queensway Christian School teachers and students who had the chance to watch Steph play when he was a teenage boy could attest to how easy he made it look to score. He scored as high as fifty points in one game during high school, and there was no denying that he consistently played a big role in the success of the Saints during his time.

The teachers and students could not forget one particular game between Queensway and Mentor College. There was approximately one-minute left and Queensway was down by eight points. The young Steph asked the coach and his teammates to pass the ball to him. Having the belief that there was a big possibility that they would lose the ball game anyway, the coach and his teammates gave in to his request. This resulted in several three-point shots which he made consecutively in a span of one minute, not to mention a couple of steals that he himself made. In the end, Queensway defeated Mentor.

While Steph became known as a three-point shooter during his teenage years, it was also during this time when he further developed his other basketball skills. He also played for the Toronto 5-0 and had the opportunity to play against Kelly Olynyk and Cory Joseph, who both eventually played in NBA as well.

However, fate did not leave Steph and his family any choice but to leave Canada and return to Charlotte, North Carolina. There, he continued to do what he loved most.

Chapter 2: Steph's Heightened Passion for Basketball

In Charlotte, North Carolina, Steph continued to exhibit his stellar basketball skills while playing on the varsity team of the Charlotte Christian School. At fifteen years old, he was a freshman who weighed less than one hundred thirty pounds, and was approximately 5'6" in height.

His first time playing for the school was in 2003 when Charlotte Christian School played against the Ravenscroft School. With his skinny frame, his jersey could practically pass for a nightgown. His team was losing the game, late in the second half. Steph gathered enough confidence to successfully take and make a three-point shot. This allowed his team to lead, and eventually win the game. Undoubtedly, his winning performance greatly impressed Knights' coach Shonn Brown.

Around this time, Steph's father also realized how genuinely serious he was about basketball. This paved the way for Dell to start mentoring his son to prepare him just in case he truly wanted to pursue a career in professional basketball.

Dell knew that aside from outstanding basketball skills, Steph also possessed an unbelievable work ethic at such a young age. Steph could dribble, shoot, and move magnificently, and he never negatively reacted to referee calls that were deemed unfair by some.

However, despite all of these positives, Dell nonetheless noticed some flaws with the way his son played basketball, particularly when it came to the fundamentals. There was no doubt that

Steph could accurately shoot the ball, but he would always shoot the ball from the hip – an ugly shot that could be easily blocked. Dell helped his son to improve his shooting form, and make it look more professional.

Having an NBA player for a father and mentor, Steph would naturally obey what Dell instructed him to do. Steph would then regularly practice on their half court at home, perfecting his shooting form. It was a big challenge for him since he was so used to his original form – he'd had it ever since he was a young kid. In fact, he considered it as something that was part of his nature, so much so that it was difficult to change or take out of his system. However, he also knew that if he wanted to truly excel as a basketball player, he should be open-minded when it came to changing habits.

Dell described Steph as someone who always got teary-eyed every time he practiced his shooting form. He just couldn't get it right and he couldn't hide his frustration. However, what was great about him was that despite such a challenge, he never gave up. He continuously practiced until he mastered the ideal shot that his father adamantly instructed him to do.

After months of training with his dad, he finally mastered his form of a quick release jump shot.

He made this transformation during his sophomore year. Little did he know that this new shooting form he had developed would later on be recognized as one of the best used in the history of basketball.

Indeed, changing habits – from hip jump shots to low-lift jump shots – paid off for Steph. He started bagging Most Valuable Player awards in high school. He helped Charlotte Christian win triple conference championships. He averaged approximately eighteen points in each game and scored one thousand four hundred basketball points in high school alone.

However, despite his outstanding performances, there was not a single major conference college that offered him a scholarship. Most, if not all, basketball recruiters deemed him to be too short and skinny.

Steph was not included in the top one hundred fifty recruits list announced by sports websites including Rivals Basketball and ESPN. He was considered a three-star recruit only and was given low scores by basketball scouts – which included well renowned basketball analyst Eric Bossi.

They noticed his flawless shots and good work ethic, but they all focused on his body frame. According to them, a man weighing one hundred eighty pounds at just six feet tall just did not look like an ideal college basketball player.

While Steph stopped hoping for major conference schools to offer him a scholarship, he considered entertaining scholarship options offered by mid-major conference colleges. He initially wanted to study at Virginia Tech where both his parents studied but, dismally, he was not offered a full scholarship. He was offered a partial scholarship by coach Seth Greenberg, but Steph opted to choose from the mid-major schools that offered him full scholarships. Among these were Winthrop University, Virginia Commonwealth University, and Davidson College. He ultimately decided to play for the Davidson Wildcats.

Chapter 3: Steph's College Basketball Career

It didn't come as a big surprise when Steph became recognized as the star player of Davidson College, where he played for three years. Whatever skills he acquired and applied when he was in grade school and high school, he was able to successfully showcase them in college basketball. Aside from that, it was noticeable how he kept on improving one year after another. Throughout his basketball life at Davidson College, there were quite a number of unforgettable moments for Steph. Truly, he left a mark as a player of Davidson Wildcats.

On his first day at Davidson College, he was just like any other ordinary new student. Despite his stellar basketball skills, the majority of the faculty and students of Davidson College had never heard of Stephen Curry.

Despite not having many people believe in his ability to reach the NBA, Steph was blessed to have a great support system. Aside from his parents and siblings, Davidson Wildcats' head coach Robert "Bob" McKillop was one of those who saw and believed in Steph's capabilities. Bob did not care if other colleges and universities thought of Steph as short, lanky, and frail. What they failed to see was his resiliency, his grit, and his heart which Bob was able to clearly see. With such great qualities, Bob knew that Steph was traversing the correct road towards success.

Steph's First Year in College Basketball

Despite the possibility that Steph could be the star player that the Davidson Wildcats had been waiting for, Bob did not give him any special treatment. In fact, when Steph arrived late on the very first day of basketball practice, Bob did not allow him to practice and asked him to go home instead. After that happened, Steph made sure that he would always arrive early for practice. As he got more and more serious about improving his craft, Steph found himself to always be the last one to leave the practice facility.

It was in November 2006 when Steph played for the Davidson Wildcats for the very first time. The basketball match was against the Eastern Michigan Eagles. He recorded a forty two percent field goal percentage and a forty three percent three-point percentage. Aside from his accurate shooting, he had several steals, assists, and rebounds that greatly contributed to their victory on that day. However, Bob noticed Steph's weakness when it came to ball control as he had thirteen turnovers in that game. This was something they would be sure to work on.

When the Wildcats played against the Michigan Wolverines in the next game, Steph was able to remarkably cut his turnovers to just three. It was unfortunate that the Wildcats lost by ten points, but the skills that Steph showcased caught the attention of everyone who watched the game. He scored thirty-two points with four assists and nine rebounds. His field goal percentage was forty eight percent.

The following game, the Wildcats played against the basketball team of Central Connecticut State in which they emerged victorious by twenty-seven points. Steph's three-point percentage was a remarkable sixty percent. He also had one block, three steals, five assists, and six rebounds.

Three days later, on November 15, 2006, Steph once again helped Davidson College win the game, this time it was against the University of Illinois-Chicago in which they won by eleven points. Their final score was one hundred points; twenty-seven of which belonged to Steph.

On November 19, 2006, however, the Davidson Wildcats lost to the Missouri Tigers by six points. It also seemed like Steph lost his momentum on that day for some reason, with a field goal percentage of only thirty six percent. He only scored sixteen points but nonetheless had four steals, four rebounds, and four assists.

Two days later, their game against Colby College was a success. The final score was 99-69, twenty-nine points of which were Steph's. However, four days later, the Davidson Wildcats lost against the Duke Blue Devils. His personal score was shockingly less than ten points. His three-point percentage was only seventeen percent while his field goal percentage was only twenty two percent.

Despite the losses, Bob did not lose faith in his team, nor in Steph. He knew that the Wildcats were simply experiencing an adjustment period. True enough, beginning December 2006, victories transpired one after another.

On December 1, the Davidson Wildcats defeated the Elon Phoenix with a final score of 86-61. Steph's personal score was eleven points.

On December 4, Curry scored twenty-four points this time in which his field goal percentage was forty-one percent. Out of his nine attempts from behind the 3-point line, four were successful. This was a close basketball game against the University of North Carolina Greensboro Spartans team, where the Wildcats won by just three points.

On December 9, the Davidson Wildcats emerged victorious in their game against the Charlotte 49ers. The final score was 79-51 in which seventeen points were contributed by Steph.

On December 15, they defeated the Mount St. Mary's Mountaineers basketball team with a final score of 116-55. During this particular game, Steph's three-point percentage was sixty percent. He also scored twenty points and made four rebounds.

On December 18, they once again emerged victorious, this time, it was against the Chattanooga Mocs basketball team. With the Wildcats winning by twelve points, Steph made three steals, six assists, eleven rebounds, and a total score of thirty points. Out of his twenty-one attempts, he made eleven field goals, and out of his thirteen 3-point shot attempts, he made six.

It was another victory for them on December 21 when they played against the Ohio Bobcats team in which Steph's score was nineteen points. On December 22, they experienced victory once again and this time it was against the Arizona State Sun Devils team. They won by five points, with Steph only scoring ten for the game. Nonetheless, it was a big deal for them as they were able to defeat a major conference school.

The last basketball match they played for that month was against the Western Michigan Broncos in which the Wildcats won by seven points. Steph scored twenty-three points, despite shooting poorly from the floor.

The Southern Conference began in January 2007 and Davidson College became a favorite for the very first time. Much was being expected from the Davidson Wildcats, with many rooting for them to be included in the championship tournament of the NCAA.

The first victorious basketball match of the Davidson Wildcats was against the College of Charleston Cougars on January 6, 2007. Steph scored nineteen points and had two rebounds. For a change, it was not Steph who scored the highest in this game, but his teammate named Thomas Sander who had a double-double with ten rebounds and twenty-five points.

On January 10, the Wildcats once again emerged victorious after they defeated the Furman Paladins by eight points. In this game, it was Thomas who led the team with twenty-four points. He was followed by another teammate named Jason Richards who scored eighteen points, who was then followed by Steph with fifteen points.

On January 13, The Wildcats won against the Wofford Terriers by five points in a game which Steph made four assists, six rebounds, and had a total score of sixteen points. Indeed, victories kept on coming one game after another as they once again experienced triumph on January 16 in a game against the Citadel Bulldogs. The Wildcats won by twenty-five points, and Steph made a couple of steals, three assists, and had four rebounds.

On January 20, 2007, however, the Davidson Wildcats experienced their first defeat in a long time when they played against the Appalachian State Mountaineers. The Wildcats lost by seven-points, despite Steph contributing fifteen. However, he only made one successful three-point shot out of his eleven attempts. His field goal percentage for this particular game was thirty-five percent. Despite the loss, the Wildcats were still positive that they would experience victories in their succeeding games.

On January 23, 2007, the Davidson Wildcats played against the Western Carolina Catamounts and won by twenty points. Steph made eight field goals out of his eleven attempts, and scored a total of twenty-five points.

On January 30, Steph scored twenty-five points again, but this time, the Wildcats played against the Elon Phoenix team. The final score was 88-58 in which Steph made eight rebounds and had nine successful field goals out of his seventeen attempts.

On February 3, 2007, the Davidson Wildcats once again played against the University of North Carolina Greensboro Spartans, and won by ten points. Steph scored twenty-nine points in this game.

On February 6, they defeated the Chattanooga Mocs for the second time with a final score of 87-57. In this game, Steph scored twenty-four points. He made the same number of points on February 12 when the Wildcats defeated the Charleston Cougars.

Then, the Western Carolina Catamounts lost against the Wildcats on February 17, with Steph scoring twenty-five points. Their next game was on February 19 against the Wofford Terriers wherein the Wildcats won by seven points. Steph scored twenty-eight points in this game.

On February 22, Steph scored twenty-four points when the Wildcats played against the Furman Paladins. They won by eighteen points and Steph contributed four assists and six rebounds.

On February 24, the Wildcats defeated the Citadel Bulldogs for the second time. With a final score of 87-70, Steph scored eighteen points.

To sum it up, Davidson College only had one loss during the Southern Conference, but they needed to emerge victorious in their succeeding games in order to qualify for the conference tournament. In that tournament, the winner would automatically earn a bid to participate in the National Championship tournament of the NCAA. This, of course, meant a lot for Davidson College – and for Steph as well.

On March 1, 2007, the Davidson Wildcats played against the Chattanooga Mocs, and won by ten points. Steph scored twenty points and made three steals, four assists, and five rebounds.

On March 2, the Wildcats once again triumphed in their game against the Furman Paladins. Steph's field goal percentage was sixty-four percent and his three-point percentage was sixty percent.

On March 3, the Wildcats won against the Charleston Cougars with a final score of 72-65. In this game, Steph scored twenty-nine points with a field goal percentage of forty-two percent. Furthermore, it was the first time that Steph played for forty minutes.

These victories allowed the Davidson Wildcats to be welcomed to the NCAA tournament. Their success in the Southern

Conference gave them the opportunity to play against the Maryland Terrapins, a team that made it to the tournament after their success in the Atlantic Coast Conference.

Sadly, on March 15, 2007, the Wildcats lost to the Terrapins with a final score of 82-70. But despite that, Steph's statistics were nonetheless impressive. He scored a total of thirty points with thirty-six percentage shooting from 3, and a forty-three percent field goal accuracy overall. Aside from him, the only other player who scored in the double digits was Jason Richards with eleven points.

Despite the loss, Davidson College was nonetheless thankful that they earned a bid in the NCAA tournament after roughly forty years. The journey to the NCAA Championship was still considered by the Davidson Wildcats a success, especially with Steph Curry around. Since his arrival, he had been able to play in all thirty-four games with an average of twenty-two points. He scored a total of seven-hundred-and-thirty points during his entire freshman year, in which three-hundred-and-sixty-six points were made through his 3-point shooting.

Steph's success as a freshman basketball player led to an opportunity for him to participate at the FIBA Under-19 World Championship, when he was chosen to become a United States representative. He also received several awards including, but not limited to, the Tournament Most Valuable Player (MVP) Award, and the Southern Conference Freshman of the Year Award.

But during this time in the NCAA, the most popular student player was Kevin Durant. Kevin was undoubtedly known as the highest scoring rookie – and Steph was the second.

Steph's Third Year in College Basketball

With his accomplishments during his freshman and sophomore years at Davidson College, he had proven that he was ready to join the NBA. However, his decision was to still play for Davidson one last time – and so he went on to be part of the Davidson Wildcats for another year.

While playing for Davidson for a third year, he used the opportunity to further hone his skills in preparation for NBA. The first basketball match played by the Davidson Wildcats was held on November 14, 2008 and it was against Guilford. Steph astonishingly collected ten assists and scored twenty-nine points. The Wildcats won by twenty-four points.

Their second game was held on November 17, 2008 and it was against the James Madison Dukes. Again, the Wildcats won with a final score of 99-64. In this game, Steph scored thirty-three points and made four steals and nine assists. He made four 3-point shots out of his six attempts, and also made fourteen field goals out of his nineteen attempts.

The Davidson Wildcats' third game was held the next day, and this time they lost to the Oklahoma Sooners by four points. Nonetheless, Steph incredibly scored forty-four points in which his 3-point shooting percentage was forty percent and his field goal percentage was forty-one percent.

On November 21, 2008, the Davidson Wildcats once again emerged victorious. This time, the basketball game was against the Winthrop Eagles. To help his team win by twenty-seven points, Steph amazingly recorded three steals and thirteen assists. All in all, his 3-point shooting percentage was forty-two percent and his field goal percentage was fifty percent.

On November 24, 2008, the Davidson Wildcats won against the Florida Atlantic Owls by sixteen points. Steph scored thirty-nine points with one block, four assists, and four rebounds. His 3-point percentage was fifty-six percent and his field goal percentage was sixty-two percent.

Apparently, Steph seemed to be consistently exhibiting stellar performances on the court. Despite this, he was just like any other star player who would experience bad shooting days once in a while. Just like on November 25, 2008, which Steph could consider as one of his worst performances. His playing time was thirty-two minutes, but he did not make a single point. Nonetheless, the Davidson Wildcats won that match against the Loyola Greyhounds by thirty points.

Steph redeemed himself during the following game on December 6, 2008 against the North Carolina State Wolfpack. Their final score was seventy-two, forty-four of which were contributed by Steph, along with two rebounds, three assists, and three steals.

On December 9, 2008, the Davidson Wildcats played against the West Virginia Mountaineers. Steph made ten assists, two blocks, four steals, four rebounds, and a total score of twenty-seven points. It was a difficult game, but the Wildcats emerged victorious by three points.

On December 13, 2008, the Wildcats played and won against the Chattanooga Mocs by five points. Their final score was one hundred points, forty-one of which belonged to Steph. His 3-point percentage was forty-six percent, while his field goal percentage was fifty percent. He also made four rebounds and six assists.

December 20, 2008 was not their day as the Wildcats lost to the Purdue Boilermakers by eighteen points. Steph scored just thirteen points, but also recorded six assists and eight rebounds.

The Wildcats once again experienced triumph when they played against the Charleston Cougars on December 29, 2008 – it was their last game for the year. It was a close game, with the Wildcats ultimately winning by only four points. As expected, Steph contributed big time to the game with three steals, seven rebounds, and nine assists. His total score was twenty-nine points.

The Wildcats' first game in 2009 was held on January 3 and it was against the Samford Bulldogs. Steph made twenty-one points, but also recorded one block, four steals, four rebounds, and eight assists. The final score was 76-55, in favor of the Wildcats.

On January 7, 2009, however, the Wildcats were defeated by the Duke Blue Devils by twelve points. Steph scored twenty-nine points and had an impressive performance with six assists and eight rebounds. However, he only made one out of his eight 3-point shot attempts.

The Wildcats' third game for 2009 was held on January 10 and it was against the Citadel Bulldogs. The final score was 84-69 and it was in favor of the Wildcats. Steph made five steals, five assists, six rebounds, and a total score of thirty-two points.

The Wildcats' next match was against the Elon Phoenix and it was held on January 14, 2009. Steph scored thirty-nine points. His 3-point percentage was sixty percent and his field goal percentage was sixty-one percent. The Wildcats won by fifteen points.

On January 21, 2009, the Wildcats played against the Furman Paladins. The Wildcats dominated, and won by forty points. Steph contributed five steals, five assists, and a total score of thirty points. His field goal percentage was sixty-seven percent.

The Wildcats then played against the Wofford Terriers on January 24, 2009 and won by twenty-three points. Steph earned a total score of thirty-three points and made seven assists, and seven rebounds.

On January 28, 2009, the Wildcats played and won against the Chattanooga Mocs by twenty-two points. Steph dropped a total of thirty-two points, with five rebounds and eight assists. It was their last game of the month.

The Wildcats' first game in February 2009 was held on the second day of the month. It was against the Western Carolina Catamounts and the Wildcats won by twenty-four points. They made eighty-nine points, twenty-six of which belonged to Steph. He also had eight assists and eight rebounds.

On February 5, 2009, the Wildcats played against the University of North Carolina Greensboro Spartans. The final score was 75-54 and it was in favor of the Wildcats. Steph contributed eight rebounds and scored a total of twenty-nine points.

Unfortunately, on February 7, 2009, the Wildcats lost to the Charleston Cougars by merely two points. Steph scored twenty-five points but he admitted that he and his teammates struggled in this particular game. His field goal percentage was just thirty percent.

On February 12, 2009, however, the Wildcats once again experienced victory and this time it was against the Wofford Terriers, with a final score of 78-61. Steph made thirty-nine points and his field goal percentage was fifty-eight percent. He also successfully made five 3-point shots out of his eight attempts.

On February 25, 2009, the Wildcats once again played against the University of North Carolina Greensboro Spartans. The final score was 70-49 and it was in favor of the Wildcats. Steph only scored twenty points, but he also had ten rebounds.

During this time, Steph made several notable achievements for himself aside from helping the Davidson Wildcats bag crucial victories. After playing eighty-three games for Davidson College, Steph was able to successfully surpass the two-thousand-point mark. He was also then recognized as the second-leading scorer in the history of Davidson College – John Gerdy being number one. He had not yet completed his junior year and yet he already had all these achievements.

On February 28, 2009, Steph became the highest scorer in the history of Davidson College when he helped the Wildcats win a game against the Georgia Southern Eagles.

On March 2, 2009, the Wildcats played against the Elon Phoenix. The Wildcats won by twelve points and had a final score of ninety points, twenty-six of which belonged to Steph. He also had three rebounds, four steals, and five assists.

By this time, it was evident that Steph and the entire team had impressed everyone in the NCAA with their remarkable performances. During Steph's junior year, the Davidson Wildcats had won eighteen games and only lost two games. But these accomplishments were not enough for them to earn a slot in the basketball tournament of the NCAA. Despite this disappointing news, the Wildcats continued to do their best in their succeeding basketball matches.

On March 7, 2009, the Wildcats played against the Appalachian State Mountaineers, in which the Wildcats won by fourteen points. Steph's field goal percentage was sixty-one percent, and his score totaled forty-three points.

On March 8, 2009, however, the Wildcats unfortunately lost once again to the Charleston Cougars by seven points. Steph's field goal percentage in this game was only twenty-eight percent and his final score totaled just twenty points.

Despite not being invited to the championship tournament of the NCAA, the Davidson Wildcats were able to participate in the National Invitational Tournament (NIT) in which they were recognized as the sixth best team.

On March 17, 2009, the Wildcats played their first NIT game and it was against the South Carolina Gamecocks. Steph scored a total of thirty-two points and his field goal percentage was forty-seven percent. They ultimately won the game by seven points.

The Wildcats' next game was held on March 23, 2009, and it was against the Saint Mary's Gaels. Steph contributed twenty-six points along with his two steals, five assists, and nine rebounds. However, the Wildcats were defeated by the Gaels.

Despite such a loss, Steph had impressive statistics at the completion of his college career. He was eventually recognized as first-team consensus of the NCAA All-American division.

By the end of his junior year, Steph had played a total of one-hundred-and-four games with the Davidson Wildcats. His statistics included an average of twenty-five points, six assists, and five rebounds per game. His 3-point shots totaled to four-hundred-and-fourteen points, and his overall points scored totaled to over two-thousand-five-hundred points. With such kind of statistics, it was evident that Steph was ready to join the NBA.

Most players don't hesitate to leave their College as early as possible if they have a chance to enter the NBA. It was a different case with Steph who still opted to stay until he completed his junior year.

In fact, even after he finished his junior year in college, he found it difficult to leave Davidson College – but he had to. The first person who knew about Steph's decision was, of course, Coach Bob.

Davidson College definitely considered Steph as one of its best players, if not the best. Through his outstanding performances, Steph helped Davidson become known nationwide. At the same time, Davidson was able to give Steph a big opportunity to hone his skills and ultimately achieve his dream of playing in the NBA.

Steph entered the NBA draft in 2009, and was selected in the first round by the Golden State Warriors.

Chapter 4: Living His Dream

Steph was recognized as the best player in the history of Davidson College. Moreover, his overall statistics as a college basketball player allowed him to bag multiple medals and awards. This simply meant that right after he completed his junior year in college, it was high time for him to join the NBA. He was indeed on the right path when he claimed eligibility for the draft in 2009.

Steph was only one hundred eight pounds and had a height of six feet and three inches when he attended the NBA draft in 2009. His weight and height had definitely improved a lot as compared to his weight and height in high school, but still, he was considered skinny and short for an NBA player.

Nonetheless, the NBA officials, members, and crew did not eliminate the fact that Steph could also emerge as a deadly NBA player. They initially compared him to a former NBA player named Chris Wayne Jackson who converted to Islam in 1991 and decided to change his name to Mahmoud Abdul-Rauf. Mahmoud was only six feet and one inch in height, but he was a dependable point guard for his former teams including Vancouver Grizzlies, Sacramento Kings, and Denver Nuggets. His statistics were not as impressive as that of Steph's, but his creativity in helping his team score baskets was remarkable and comparable to that of Steph's playing style.

When it came to skills, there was no denying that Steph could be considered a complete package. With his intense shooting and ball-handling skills, it was not surprising that those who watched him play were often left in awe. Despite having bad days, he nonetheless consistently displayed his extraordinary athletic performance as a college basketball player.

His skills were also compared to that of Ray Allen's and Reggie Miller's. Ray and Reggie were also regarded as two of the most lethal shooters in NBA history. Like them, Steph was skillful in finding open spots where he could successfully take shots.

There was no denying that Steph was a consistent shooter. However, he knew that aside from being a shooter, he also had to learn the other aspects of being a well-rounded professional basketball player. He was so used to being a shooting guard because that was his position when he was in college, but he knew he had to learn the skills of a point guard also.

Besides, if he was to join the NBA, he had to become an expert point guard because his height and weight were not ideal for a shooting guard as far as professional basketball is concerned.

In college, Steph was not trained to become the playmaker. His role was to be a secondary ball-handler. His major role was to find open spots and successfully shoot the ball.

Despite being a shooting guard in college, Steph was already exhibiting important skills needed to become a great point guard player. This was observed by Stevan Petrovic, an NBA scout, who had the opportunity to watch Steph play college basketball several times.

Petrovic said that he had seen Steph become a playmaker in several matches and that Steph was not at all selfish as a playmaker. Steph was skillful in making great passes and in making fast and appropriate decisions while on the court. Petrovic had also observed how Steph never seemed to get pressured on the court. He always looked cool despite the presence of defensive pressure. Perhaps, his calmness was what helped him make great and quick decisions while on the court.

As mentioned, since he was not tall and did not have a big body frame, it was anticipated that he would not stand out in the NBA. What everyone in the NBA did not anticipate was the fact that his weight and height would nonetheless be an advantage as a defensive player. In fact, in college, one of his best skills was stealing the ball.

During the first few NBA games played by Steph, he was being bullied on the court by bigger guards such as Dwyane Wade and Kobe Bryant. Steph was anticipated to always attempt to make pull-up jumpers because of his inability to go near the basket. He was also anticipated to not easily draw fouls because his small body frame made it easy for opponents to avoid him.

Since he was small for a shooting guard, he was trained to be an NBA point guard. However, he was still way smaller than many other point guards in the league.

His lack of size made it difficult for him to guard players such as Manu Ginobili, Dwyane Wade, and Kobe Bryant. Furthermore, in terms of speed, he couldn't match the quickness of Devin Harris, Derrick Rose, and Chris Paul.

Evidently, many NBA people did not see that much potential in Steph. If there was any advantage for drafting him, they all thought that it would lie in his shooting skills and nothing more.

When Curry attended the NBA Draft in 2009, he seemed to be emotionally prepared. He knew what most people thought of him and of his capabilities. He knew that there were a lot of people who were questioning his future in the NBA. He knew he had a lot of skills to improve upon, but at the time all he wanted was to simply be drafted.

The 2009 NBA Draft was considered to be one of the weakest draft classes since 2000, during which the top pick was Kenyon Martin who initially played for the New Jersey Nets.

Blake Griffin, the star player of Oklahoma University, was the favorite entering the draft. That was why it didn't come as a surprise that the Los Angeles Clippers made him their first draft pick. Everyone knew that Blake had the potential to become a future All-Star player.

James Harden, the star player of Arizona State University, was picked number 2 by the Oklahoma City Thunder to be their shooting guard. The Thunder's plan was to create a trio, and James was drafted to join Kevin Durant and Russell Westbrook.

Tyreke Evans was the star player of Memphis University and was picked next by the Sacramento Kings. The team badly needed a point guard at that time, and they saw the potential of Tyreke.

Hasheem Thabeet, the University of Connecticut star player, was drafted next by the Memphis Grizzlies. He became popular in college basketball due to his outstanding ability to block shots. Unfortunately, he had a difficult time replicating such success in the NBA.

Despite the fact that the Minnesota Timberwolves could get both Ricky Rubio and Steph, the team opted to get Ricky only.

Ricky was known to possess the same stellar skills as that of the former NBA player Pete Maravich.

With the next pick, the Timberwolves still did not pick Steph. Instead, they chose Jonny Flynn from Syracuse University. Had they picked Steph, the team could have had an amazing starting five that would also include Ricky Rubio, Kevin Love, and DeMarcus Cousins. The team's refusal to pick Steph stemmed from Steph's refusal to attend one of the team's training sessions prior to the draft. Steph's decision was due to the questionable status of Kevin McHale. At the time, it wasn't clearly established is McHale was the official coach of the team or not. Steph simply voiced out his concern that he did not want to start training with a team that did not have an official coach yet. Unfortunately, such a decision was received poorly by the Timberwolves.

While most NBA teams chose to not pick Steph, the New York Knicks were one of the teams that were interested in drafting him. The team badly needed a shooter, especially after Quentin Richardson and Jamal Crawford parted ways with the team. Besides, Coach Mike D'Antoni saw the potential of Steph. The team was certain that they wanted to pick Steph, but they still had to wait for their turn as the eighth pick.

In the draft order, the Golden State Warriors was in the seventh overall position and the team made such an unexpected move when they picked Steph. Being picked by the Warriors meant that he would join Monta Ellis and Jamal Crawford, two undersized shooting guards. Sadly, the decision to pick Steph was booed by the disappointed fans who went to the arena to watch the draft live. The fans were expecting that the Warriors would make a strong pick as it was an opportunity to save their struggling team.

So, when the Golden State Warriors announced that they had selected Stephen Curry, it apparently came as a surprise to the fans and to the entire NBA. Steph was vocal that he did not want to form part of the Warriors team. In fact, the team's general manager Larry Riley even invited Steph, through his agent Jeff Austin, to join a Warriors workout prior to the draft. But Steph politely turned it down because he was only interested in playing for the New York Knicks. Steph believed that his skills were well suited for the team. However, Larry was so impressed with his skills that he was determined to pick him. Larry had seen Steph play several times and could not help but compare him to Steve Nash.

Larry did not have much of a hard time convincing Don Nelson, the Warriors head coach at the time. Jeff already had an inkling that the Warriors might pick Steph, so he told Larry about his and Steph's plans of playing for the Knicks. In fact, Steph's father, Dell, also had a hunch that the Warriors would pick him. Dell was actually hoping that Larry would change his mind last minute.

After being drafted, there were uncertainties as to how Steph would fit in with his new team. Monta, just like Steph, was also small for a shooting guard. At times, Monta would also play as the team's point guard. The two players possessed very similar skillsets. It seemed difficult to imagine how the future tandem could beat bigger opponents. Furthermore, with Monta and Jamal playing shooting and point guards for the Warriors, there was possibility that Steph might not be given much playing time.

Surprisingly though, on draft day, Larry agreed to trade Jamal to the Atlanta Hawks for Speedy Claxton and Acie Law.

Steph as a Rookie Player

Soon after being drafted, Steph was instructed to sign a contract in July 2009. It was a contract for four years that was worth approximately thirteen-million U.S. dollars. The amount offered to him was, in fact, slightly higher than what was normally offered to rookie players.

He was then instructed to be the team's point guard while Monta was to be the shooting guard. The tandem was undersized, but Larry and Don predicted them to be dynamic.

The very first NBA game played by Steph as a Warriors point guard was against the Houston Rockets on October 28, 2009. On that day, there was heavy traffic and Steph arrived at the venue a little late, but nonetheless just in time for the game.

The NBA crewmen immediately approached Steph as soon as he arrived and even fans were asking for his autograph. He kind of felt awkward and uncomfortable with all the attention he was getting because, in his mind, these people had not even seen him play yet. He also felt pressured as the fans and the media both seemed to be expecting a lot from him.

When the Warriors players were finally instructed to enter the court, the veterans asked Steph to go first and they would follow. However, it was a traditional prank played by the veterans in which they would let the rookie run all by himself and not join him on the basketball court. Just like the rest, Steph fell for the prank.

It was unfortunate that the Warriors lost to Houston by one point. Nonetheless, Steph succeeded in making a good first impression on the team, the fans, and the entire NBA community. He scored a total of fourteen points and made four steals and seven assists. He successfully made seven field goals out of his twelve attempts.

It was Steph's first NBA game and, unfortunately, his first loss. Apparently, he could not hide his disappointment about it. His statistics on that day were quite impressive for a rookie but, according to Steph, he was not able to give his all as he was exceedingly nervous to play professional basketball for the very first time. Nonetheless, he exuded calmness while on the playing court.

Just like any other rookie player, Steph didn't have any choice but to quickly adjust to the schedule of professional basketball. Steph had gotten used to the schedule of college basketball in which approximately thirty-five games were played in a span of six months. In one NBA season, they had to play eighty-two games in a span of six months.

During Steph's first month as a rookie player, not a lot of offensive opportunities were opening up and his final scores were mostly in the single digits. However, things improved in November 2009 when scored an average of nineteen points per game. On December 7, 2009, he scored twenty-two points for the first time when the team played against the Oklahoma City Thunder. Steph had two assists, four steals, four rebounds, and his field goal percentage was sixty-four percent. In this particular game, however, the one who led the team was still Monta Ellis. Monta scored thirty-one points with a field goal percentage of forty-three percent. Despite Steph's and Monta's good performances, it was unfortunate that the Warriors still lost to Oklahoma by sixteen points.

On December 18, 2009, the Warriors experienced another loss and this time it was against the Washington Wizards. Nonetheless, Steph scored a total of twenty-seven points with eight rebounds, three steals, and four assists. His 3-point percentage was fifty-six percent, while his field goal percentage was fifty-three percent.

On December 23, 2009, the Warriors experienced another loss against the New Orleans Hornets wherein the final score was 108-102. Out of the Warriors' final score of one-hundred-and-two, seventeen points belonged to Steph. He also had an impressive ten rebounds.

On January 5, 2010, the Warriors once again lost, and this time it was in a match against the Denver Nuggets. The final score only had a one-point difference and Steph scored a total of twenty-six points. He also recorded three steals, six assists, and five rebounds.

It was unfortunate that during their next games, Monta could not play due to a minor injury. Such an unfortunate event could also be perceived as a blessing in disguise as Steph had the opportunity to further showcase his basketball skills. True enough, on January 23, 2010, Steph showed that he was also capable of leading the team as the Warriors won against the New Jersey Nets. Aside from scoring a total of thirty-two points, he also had four steals and seven assists. He scored seven out of his eight free throw attempts, and scored eleven out of his twenty-one field goal attempts.

On February 10, 2010, still without Monta, the Warriors emerged victorious by thirty points in their game against the Los Angeles Clippers. Steph, for the first time, had a triple-double. He impressed everyone with his final score of thirty-six points with ten rebounds and thirteen assists. He successfully made seven 3-point shots out of his eleven attempts. Based on his overall performances from the time he first played for the Warriors until that game against the Clippers, Steph had scored an average of twenty-two points per game. His average 3-point shot percentage was forty-three percent, and his field goal percentage was forty-six percent.

Steph's impressive performance gave him the opportunity to be included in the All-Star event that was held on February 13, 2010. At the American Airlines Center located in Dallas, Texas, he formed part of the three-point shootout category in which his opponents included Channing Frye of the Phoenix Suns and Chauncey Billups of the Detroit Pistons. The mechanics were simple, each player simply had to make as many successful shots as possible from the three-point perimeter. There were five stations with a total of five basketballs per station. The first four basketballs were worth one point each while the last ball – which was called the "money ball" – was worth two points. This meant that the player who could successfully shoot all twenty-five basketballs would score a total of thirty points. Steph scored eighteen points which allowed him to advance to the final round. In the final round, Paul Pierce of the Boston Celtics won first place with a total of twenty points. Steph made it to second place with seventeen points and Chauncey finished in third place with fourteen points.

On February 12, 2010, Steph also had the opportunity to participate in the NBA Rookie Challenge, an event held by the

NBA on an annual basis. In this event, the top rookie players compete in a special exhibition game against second-year NBA players. Steph's teammates included Tyreke Evans of the Sacramento Kings, Brandon Jennings of the Milwaukee Bucks, and James Harden of the Oklahoma City Thunder. Held in Dallas, Texas, the sophomore team was defeated by the rookie team with a final score of 140-128. Steph was given a playing time of twenty-two minutes in which he scored a total of fourteen points with one rebound and two assists. He successfully made six field goals out of his eleven attempts.

On April 7, 2010, the Golden State Warriors defeated the Minnesota Timberwolves. Steph recorded seven steals, eight rebounds, fourteen assists, and twenty-seven points. In this game, his performance was recognized as the best performance by a rookie player in that year. What people did not expect was that he was just getting started.

On April 14, 2010, the Golden State Warriors once again emerged victorious after defeating the Portland Trail Blazers by six points. The Warriors scored a total of one-hundred-and-twenty-two points, forty-two of which came from Steph. His 3-point shot percentage was sixty-seven percent, and his field goal percentage was fifty-two percent. He also had eight assists and nine rebounds.

In the 2009-2010 NBA season, Blake Griffin suffered from injuries that unfortunately prevented him from playing. This paved the way for Steph to become the favorite nominee for the Rookie of the Year. During this season, the closest competition of Steph was Tyreke Evans as the latter was recognized as the third NBA rookie player in history to score an average of twenty points with five assists and five rebounds per game. Steph only had an average of seventeen points, two steals, five rebounds, and six assists per game. He ultimately only earned second place, but it gave him the opportunity to join the All-Rookie First Team in which he impressed everyone with his three-point shooting ability, steals, and assists.

During this time, the Golden State Warriors were struggling to make the playoffs. The front office staff of the team had no choice but to let go of Coach Don after the season and replace him with Keith Smart who was asked to start in the 2010-2011 season.

Prior to the start of the 2010-2011 season, the NBA community selected players to participate in the United States National Team. Evidently, Steph's efforts as a professional basketball player were paying off as he was asked to join the national team. He was grateful for such an opportunity after the disappointments he faced with his team not making the playoffs. In the national team, Steph played as a backup guard for players Derrick Rose, Russell Westbrook, Chauncey Billups, and Kobe Bryant. His best game was against Tunisia in which he scored a total of thirteen points. By the end of the tournament, Steph had an average score of five points after playing a total of nine games.

During that time, the U.S. national team coach was Michael William "Mike" Krzyzewski. Mike was one of the college basketball coaches who had rejected Steph during his quest for a scholarship. Mike was the head coach of the Duke Blue Devils and, just like how other college basketball coaches felt, he thought that Steph was too short and skinny for both college and professional basketball. However, Mike was humble enough to admit that he indeed made a mistake for underestimating the capabilities of Steph. After watching Steph play for the Warriors and the national team, Mike admitted that Steph was not only a shooter but was a playmaker as well. As time went by, Mike also learned that Steph had way more to offer in international basketball.

Despite the losses encountered by his team and only placing second in the Rookie of the Year rankings, Steph was glad about how things were turning out in his basketball career. However, it was also during this time when he experienced one of the biggest scares of his life. In March 2010, the Warriors played against the Los Angeles Lakers. He also went to the Warriors practice the very next day. Everything was normal until the day after that practice. As soon as he woke up, his ankle felt sore. He found this odd because he could not remember spraining it during the past few days. He tried to ignore the soreness and headed to the arena for a Warriors game. Prior to the game, he tried practicing some shots only to realize that he found it difficult to land on his ankle. When the team doctors checked his ankle, it was found out that it was inflamed, and he was forced to sit out.

After that experience, he eventually regained his strength and did not experience any other serious illness or injury during that season. However, he did not anticipate that such an ankle injury could have a long-term effect on him, as he would encounter same injury later on in his career.

Steph's Third NBA Season

Due to the ankle injuries he suffered during his freshman and sophomore years in the NBA, Steph had no choice but to undergo surgery to address his ankle problem. The surgery aimed to strengthen his ankle that was often injured. This prompted the Warriors to revamp their roster under their new coach Mark Jackson, who was previously an NBA point guard. The Warriors management also wanted to get DeAndre Jordan, but he was instead recruited by the Los Angeles Clippers.

On draft day, it came as a surprise when the Golden State Warriors picked Klay Thompson who played for Washington State University. Klay is the son of Mychal Thompson, a former Los Angeles Lakers player. Similar to Curry, Klay was recognized as one deadly player back in college basketball. His strengths included his shooting skills and his ability as a tough defender. NBA analysts criticized the decision of the Warriors to pick Klay. They thought that the team should have selected a big man to heavily play defense but, instead, they picked Klay.

The occurrence of a lockout at the start of the 2011-2012 NBA season resulted in a shortened season and fewer games to play for all NBA teams. In the case of the Golden State Warriors, they only had a chance to play sixty-six games. The difficult part was that the schedule was so tight that they often had to play for two or three consecutive days. It was a tedious season for the players.

The 2011-2012 season began in December. It was somehow a blessing in disguise for Steph because he had extra time to recover from his surgery – but it didn't seem to be long enough. When the Warriors played against the Sacramento Kings during a preseason game, then-rookie Jimmer Fredette crossed over Steph. This resulted in his ankle getting sprained once again. Nonetheless, he forced himself to play on that season.

On December 25, 2011, Steph only scored four points in the Warriors game against the Los Angeles Lakers. The team lost by nineteen points. However, on December 26, 2011, Steph's determination to redeem himself helped the Warriors win in a game against the Chicago Bulls by eight points. Steph scored twenty-one points with ten assists. He made six successful free throws out of his seven attempts. He also made seven successful field goals out of his twelve attempts.

On December 31, 2011, Steph scored twenty-one points once again when the Warriors played against the Philadelphia 76ers. However, it was only Steph and David Lee who scored in double digits, with Lee having a total score of nineteen points. This led to their loss against Philadelphia with a final score of 107-79.

The tandem of Steph Curry and Klay Thompson was not yet seen during this time. In fact, it took a little while before they could play together as Steph's ankle injury prevented him from playing several times. During this season, Steph was only able to play twenty-six games out of the sixty-six allotted for the Warriors.

On January 4, 2012, Steph sprained his ankle during a Warriors game against the San Antonio Spurs. This, however, occurred after he had already scored a total of twenty points and eight assists. The Warriors unfortunately lost the game by six points.

Steph returned from his ankle injury on January 20, 2012 when the Warriors played against the Indiana Pacers. He only made twelve points and his field goal percentage was thirty-three percent. The Indiana Pacers won the game by a mere three points.

On January 25, 2012, however, Steph seemed to have recovered from his injury. The Warriors played against the Portland Trail Blazers and it was Steph who led the team by scoring thirty-two points. With a playing time of thirty-eight minutes, he had four steals, six rebounds, and seven assists. This time, the Warriors emerged triumphant with a final score of 101-93.

On February 2, 2012, Steph scored a total of twenty-nine points in a Warriors game against the Utah Jazz. His field goal percentage was seventy-one percent and he recorded three steals, five rebounds, and twelve assists. The Warriors won against the Jazz by eighteen points.

On February 9, 2012, The Golden State Warriors played against the Denver Nuggets, and emerged victorious once again by eight points. Steph scored a total of thirty-six points with seven assists and seven rebounds. His field goal percentage was an incredible seventy-six percent.

On February 18, 2012, the Golden State Warriors lost to the Memphis Grizzlies by a single point. Despite the loss, it was considered as one of the team's rare games where both Steph and Monta had incredible performances. Monta earned a final score of thirty-three points and his field goal percentage was forty-six percent. At the same time, Steph scored a total of thirty-six points and his field goal percentage was sixty-two percent.

On February 22, 2012, the Golden State Warriors played against the Phoenix Suns, and won by two points. However, after having played for only ten minutes, Steph suffered another ankle sprain. During that ten-minutes of playing time, he scored nine points. Again, he had to miss the next few games.

Steph tried to play on February 29, 2012 when the Warriors played against the Atlanta Hawks. However, his ankle bothered him once again after playing for just a few seconds on the court. He was not even able to finish watching his teammates play as he needed to leave early for his treatment.

On March 5, 2012, the Warriors played against the Washington Wizards in a game they won by twenty points. Steph tried to play just to see if he could finally go back to the performing on the court. He lasted for just over nine minutes and scored twelve points.

On March 7, 2012, Steph increased his playing time to twenty minutes. Although the Golden State Warriors lost to the Memphis Grizzlies by eight points, Steph was able to record three assists, four rebounds, and fifteen points. It was during this game when Steph thought that his health was improving. He hoped to be able to play longer in the next Warriors game.

However, on March 10, 2012, Steph sprained his ankle once again when the Golden State Warriors played against the Dallas Mavericks. After playing for approximately sixteen minutes, Steph scored ten points. Fortunately, the Warriors won with a final score of 111-87.

The game between the Golden State Warriors and the Los Angeles Clippers on March 11, 2012 could be considered as one of Steph's worst games in his career in professional basketball. After playing for nine minutes, he once again experienced an ankle sprain. During his playing time, he only collected one assist and three rebounds. The Warriors nonetheless won the game by five points.

Steph had no choice but to spend the rest of the season recovering from his ankle problem. He also had to undergo another surgery at the end of the season. Nonetheless, the Warriors' general manager Bob Myers, who was newly appointed at that time, never considered letting go of Steph. The plans for the Warriors team continuously included Steph despite his proneness to injuries.

For the next season, Bob Myers decided to recruit Australian player Andrew Bogut. The Warriors also got Richard Jefferson as they traded Monta Ellis to the Milwaukee Bucks, and Stephen Jackson to the San Antonio Spurs.

The Golden State Warriors were known for replacing their head coach every season. However, this time, Mark Jackson was given the opportunity to still be the head coach for the next season – an opportunity to transform the struggling Warriors into a winning team. Besides, due to Steph's injury, a lot of unexpected events had transpired, and Mark had to adjust his coaching skills. It was understandable that he should be given another chance to coach the team.

The Golden State Warriors had been a struggling team since 2006, and Steph, in spite of being an outstanding basketball player, had not been able to exhibit his stellar skills one hundred percent since he started his career in the NBA. Had he not been plagued by injuries, he could have developed into an even better player by his third year in the NBA.

By the end of the 2011-2012 season, Steph underwent a surgery that aimed to address his ankle problem one hundred percent.

His head surgeon was Richard Ferkel who was a doctor at the California Orthopedic Institute, and who had conducted many surgical procedures that involved athletes. When Dr. Ferkel analyzed Steph's ankle problem, Dr. Ferkel decided that the initial step was to reconstruct whatever was done by Steph's previous surgeon. Dr. Ferkel aimed to make Steph's ankles feel brand new.

Steph was not certain of his future with the Golden State Warriors – most particularly, his future in the NBA in general – knowing that his rookie contract was about to end. Everything was uncertain, including whether or not the NBA community was still interested in seeing him play. At that time, Steph's future heavily relied on how successful his ankle surgery would turn out to be. He knew that it could either make or break his NBA career.

The doctors found that Steph's ankles did not have any structural damage. It was just that his ankles would get easily sprained which caused bone spurs as well as inflamed tissue. These findings fortunately shortened his recovery period from six months to four at the maximum. Three months following the surgery, Steph was prepared to undergo rehabilitation.

Steph did not waste any time as he exerted his effort to regain his health for the next season. He was determined to play in the NBA for a long time.

Steph's Fourth NBA Season

Steph's third NBA season was indeed a disappointing one both for him and the entire Warriors team. For his fourth season, the Warriors had two big players, namely, Andrew Bogut and David Lee, who were responsible for playing under the basket. They would be assisted by Steph and Klay. This was the start of the Steph-Klay team up. During the draft, the Warriors also picked Harrison Barnes, the star forward of the North Carolina Tar Heels. The Warriors team was basically composed of young players, but the team retained strong veterans like Carl Landry and Jarrett Jack. With their new line-up, the Warriors appeared to have the potential to do better this season. This fact excited Coach Mark Jackson too, especially considering that Steph was expected to be able to play without further injuries.

Steph was grateful that he would stay with the Warriors for another four seasons after signing a new contract with the team effective the 2013-2014 season. It was quite apparent that the Warriors had no intention of letting go of Steph. Furthermore, it seemed as if they could definitely foresee Steph's potential as their star player.

The contract's worth was a total of forty-four million U.S. dollars for four years. The amount was way lower than that of the other players who signed a similar contract such as DeAndre Jordan, JaVale McGee, and Tiago Splitter. Sadly, Steph's ankle injury prevented him from being offered a higher deal.

When Steph began playing in the 2012-2013 season, it was quite obvious that Coach Mark was guiding him well. On October 31, 2012, the Warriors played against the Phoenix

Suns. Despite only scoring two points in this game, Steph nonetheless had two steals, three assists, and seven rebounds. The Warriors also won by two points.

However, in their second game against the Suns, the Warriors lost by ten points. Nonetheless, Steph scored a total of twenty-six points with a fifty percent field goal percentage. He also collected five rebounds and seven assists.

On November 29, 2012, the Warriors played against the Denver Nuggets and won by one point. Steph scored a total of twenty points and made ten assists. His field goal percentage was forty-one percent.

On December 1, 2012, the Warriors played and won against the Indiana Pacers by eleven points. Steph once again scored a total of twenty points and made eleven assists. His field goal percentage was fifty percent.

The Warriors lost to the Orlando Magic on December 3, 2012. Nonetheless, Steph was able to score twenty-five points and made eleven assists. Two days later, the Warriors played against the Detroit Pistons. The Warriors won and Steph scored a total of twenty-two points. He also collected ten assists.

On December 7, 2012, the Warriors won again and this time it was against the Brooklyn Nets. Steph scored twenty-eight points and made four rebounds and five assists. His 3-point percentage was fifty-six percent and his field goal percentage was fifty-three percent.

The start of 2013 was a success for Steph as he helped his team win against the Los Angeles Clippers by twenty-one points on January 2, 2013. His 3-point percentage was seventy-five percent, while his field goal percentage was sixty-nine percent. He grabbed six rebounds, eight assists, and a final score of thirty-one points.

On January 11, 2013, Steph recorded a double-double as he made twelve assists and scored twenty-two points. This was when the Golden State Warriors played against the Portland Trail Blazers in a game that they won by six points. In this game, Steph's field goal percentage was thirty-two percent.

Steph suffered minor injuries that prevented him from playing with his team for two consecutive games. He, however, returned on January 23, 2012 in which the Warriors won by five points against the Oklahoma City Thunder. Steph scored a total of thirty-one points and collected three rebounds, four steals, and seven assists. His field goal percentage was forty-one percent. However, he suffered minor injuries once again that prevented him from playing two consecutive games.

Steph came back on February 2, 2013 to play with his team against the Phoenix Suns. The Warriors emerged victorious with a final score of 113-93. Steph successfully made two steals, two rebounds, eight assists, and scored a total of twenty-nine points. His field goal percentage was fifty-five percent.

On February 8, 2013, it was unfortunate that the Golden State Warriors lost to the Memphis Grizzlies by six points. In this game, Steph was able to score thirty-two points and recorded two steals, five rebounds, and eight assists.

Again, it was unfortunate that the Golden State Warriors lost to the New York Knicks by four points in a game held on February 27, 2013 at the Madison Square Garden in New York City. The Warriors' final score was one-hundred-and-five points, fifty-four of which belonged to Steph alone. He made three steals, six rebounds, and seven assists. Most importantly, he amazingly hit eleven 3-point shots in this game, earning the second place for the most number of 3-point shots ever made in a game. The record was held by Donyell Marshall and Kobe Bryant who both made twelve 3-point shots in one game.

Also, in February 2013, Steph dropped a total of thirty-eight points when the Warriors played against the Indiana Pacers. Furthermore, he recorded one block, a couple of rebounds, three steals, and four assists. Unfortunately, the Warriors lost this game by eleven points.

On March 1, 2013, the Boston Celtics defeated the Golden State Warriors by eight points. Nonetheless, Steph was able to make twenty-five points and six assists. On March 2, 2013, the Warriors once again lost, and this time it was against the Philadelphia 76ers. The final score was 104-97. In this game, Steph made nine assists and scored thirty points. Despite the losses, Steph was performing well as a Warriors player.

On March 4, 2013, the Warriors finally emerged victorious in their game against the Toronto Raptors with a final score of 125-118. Steph's final score was twenty-six points, on top of his five rebounds and twelve assists.

On March 9, 2013, however, the Warriors once again faced a loss and this time it was against the Milwaukee Bucks. Steph had ten assists in this game but only scored a total of sixteen points.

On March 11, 2013, the Warriors won against the New York Knicks with a final score of 92-63. Steph's stats included one steal, three assists, and six rebounds. His final score totaled to twenty-six points.

The Warriors once again won on March 13, 2013 and this time it was against the Detroit Pistons, with a final score of 105-97. Steph's field goal percentage was sixty-five percent. He had eight assists and thirty-one points by the end of the game.

The Warriors experienced another victory on March 17, 2013 as they defeated the Houston Rockets, with a final score of 108-78. Steph made eleven assists and scored twenty-nine points. He was able to successfully make twelve out of his twenty-two field goal attempts.

The Warriors was consistently performing well as they defeated the New Orleans Pelicans on March 18, 2013, with a final score of 93-72. Steph scored a total of thirty points and made three assists and seven rebounds. He successfully made ten out of his nineteen field goal attempts, as well as six successful 3-point shots out of his nine attempts.

The Golden State Warriors were in for another victory as they defeated the Washington Wizards on March 23, 2013, with a final score of 101-92. Steph's field goal percentage was an astounding seventy-two percent. He made eight assists and scored a total of thirty-five points.

On March 25, 2013, the Warriors defeated the Los Angeles Lakers this time, with a final score of 109-103. Steph had seven rebounds, ten assists, and a final score of twenty-five points.

After experiencing consecutive wins, the Warriors unfortunately lost when they played against the Sacramento

Kings on March 30, 2013. Steph scored seventeen points and made twelve assists.

By April 2013, the Warriors were doing their best to secure a spot in the playoffs. On April 3, 2013, the team won against the New Orleans Hornets with a final score of 98-88. Steph was able to record one steal, three rebounds, and nine assists. His final score was twenty points.

The victories continued, and it looked as if the Warriors would finally make the playoffs.

Steph's ability as a 3-point shooter paid off when he scored a total of two-hundred-and-seventy-two 3-pointers over the seventy-eight games he played that season. This success broke the record of Ray Allen as the most 3-pointers ever scored in a single season.

Steph's statistics by the end of the season included an average of approximately two steals, seven assists, four rebounds, and an average score of twenty-three points. His 3-point percentage was forty-five percent, as was his field-goal percent overall.

In April 2013, he received the Player of the Month award for the Western Conference for averaging twenty-five points, two steals, four rebounds, and eight assists per game. He was also praised for being one-half of the Splash Brothers, the other half of which was Klay Thompson. Indeed, Steph played an important role in helping the Warriors earn a spot in the playoffs. In the Pacific Division, the team bagged second place, while in the Western Conference, they finished in the sixth spot.

On April 20, 2013, during the NBA playoffs' opening rounds, the Warriors played against the Denver Nuggets but lost by three points, with a final score of 97-95. Steph only scored nineteen points but made four rebounds and had nine assists. His field goal percentage in this game was thirty-five percent.

On April 23, 2013, however, the Warriors won against the Nuggets, with a final score of 131-117. It was clear to everyone who watched the game that the Splash Brothers had an awesome performance. Steph scored a total of thirty points with three steals, five rebounds, and thirteen assists, whereas Klay scored twenty-one points with seventy-three percent shooting.

Game 3 was held on April 26, 2013 and the Warriors once again emerged victorious against the Nuggets, with a final score of 110-108. Steph led the game with a final score of twenty-nine points. He also made two steals, six rebounds, and eleven assists.

The Warriors once again defeated the Nuggets in Game 4 which was held on April 28, 2013, with a final score of 115-101. Steph earned thirty-one points with three rebounds, four steals, and seven assists. His 3-point shot percentage was fifty-five percent, while his field goal percentage was sixty-three percent.

However, Game 5 was won by the Nuggets as the Warriors were defeated by seven points on April 30, 2013, with a final score of 107-100. In this game, Steph only scored fifteen points but had four rebounds and eight assists.

Held on May 2, 2013, the series ended in Game 6 when the Warriors won by four points, with a final score of 92-88. Steph had two steals, four rebounds, eight assists, and his final score totaled to twenty-two points.

In the entire series between the Golden State Warriors and the Denver Nuggets, the statistics Steph averaged approximately two steals, four rebounds, nine assists, and a score of twenty-four points per game.

The next round of the playoffs was between the Golden State Warriors and the San Antonio Spurs. Game 1 was held on May 6, 2013 but, unfortunately, the Warriors lost in a double overtime match, with a final score of 129-127. Nonetheless, Steph showcased a stellar performance after scoring forty-four points with a field goal percentage of fifty-one percent. He also made two steals, four rebounds, and eleven assists.

In Game 2 that was held on May 8, 2013, the Warriors emerged victorious this time with a final score of 100-91. Steph had fourteen rebounds and scored twenty-two points. Klay also had a strong performance, scoring thirty-four points by the end of the game.

In Game 3, however, it was again the San Antonio Spurs' turn to emerge victorious, with a final score of 102-92. Held on May 10, 2013, Steph's field goal percentage was just twenty-nine percent. He only scored at total of sixteen points along with eight assists.

Game 4 was then held on May 12, 2013 in which an overtime match was won by the Warriors, with a final score of 97-87, tying the series. The team was led by Harrison Barnes who scored a total of twenty-six points and ten rebounds. Steph helped the team succeed by scoring twenty-two points, while Andrew Bogut assisted with eighteen rebounds. In these first four games of the series, Steph played an average of forty-six minutes per game.

Steph seemed to have a bad night when he only scored nine points in Game 5 which was held on May 14, 2013. To make matters worse, he also had four turnovers and a twenty-nine percent field goal percentage. The Warriors lost by eighteen points, with a final score of 109-91.

On May 16, 2013, Game 6 was won by the San Antonio Spurs. Nonetheless, Steph was able to lead the team with a total score of twenty-two points. He also made one block, one steal, four rebounds, and six assists.

The Warriors may have lost the series, but making the second round of the playoffs was an achievement in itself.

Meanwhile, it was quite evident too that Steph definitely had the potential to lead the Warriors under the guidance of Coach Mark. This meant that the Warriors had not made a mistake when they let go of Monta Ellis. They also did not go wrong when they let Steph sign a contract for four seasons. Now, their next step was to pick another star player to make the team even stronger – and so they picked Andre Tyler "Iggy" Iguodala to play small forward for the team. Iggy was not known for his shooting skills, but he was equipped with all the other basketball skills that a team needed in a player.

Steph's Fifth NBA Season

In the 2013-2014 season, the Golden State Warriors hired Keke Lyles as their performance director. Previously working for the Minnesota Timberwolves, Keke was well-known for being one of the best strength and conditioning coaches. He had become an expert in analyzing the moves of athletes as well as addressing their athletic misfortunes. Of course, he didn't hesitate to study Steph's ankle problems and to find a solution.

According to Keke, Steph had an extraordinary ability to change his pace while playing on the court. Steph was never regarded as the fastest basketball player but his ability to quickly change pace was a skill that not many could match. However, Keke noticed that Steph heavily depended on his ankle every time he would quickly change his pace. Keke said that Steph could address this by learning to rely on his hips instead of his ankles when quickly changing his pace.

When Keke told Steph of how his ankle problem could be addressed, Steph open-mindedly listened to and obeyed Keke's strength and conditioning program. When Steph was told that he needed to initially learn several yoga poses to develop his overall balance, he worked double time to learn those poses. Keke was in awe of Steph's work ethic.

On October 31, 2013, the Golden State Warriors lost their first game for the season to the Los Angeles Lakers, with a final score of 126-115. Nonetheless, Steph amazingly scored thirty-eight points and made nine assists. His 3-point shooting percentage was sixty-four percent, and his field goal percentage was sixty-one percent. It was just the start a tremendous season for Steph.

On December 9, 2013, the Warriors unfortunately lost to the Charlotte Bobcats, with a final score of 115-111. Steph's score, however, was an amazing forty-three points, along with a couple of blocks, six rebounds, and nine assists. His total field goal percentage was forty-four percent.

On January 31, 2014, Steph scored a total of forty-four points in a Warriors game against the Utah Jazz. He made fourteen successful field goals out of his twenty-six attempts. He also made eight successful 3-point shots out of his thirteen attempts. The Warriors won this time, with a final score of 95-90.

On April 13, 2014, Steph had a standout performance. He earned a total of forty-seven points, and his field goal percentage was fifty-five percent. He successfully made seven 3-point shots out of his fourteen attempts.

On November 4, 2013, when the Warriors won against the Philadelphia 76ers, Steph had a triple-double with ten rebounds, twelve assists, and a final score of eighteen points. He also recorded one block, five steals, and a field goal percentage of forty-four percent. The final score of the game was 110-90.

On December 27, 2013, Steph had another triple-double performance when the Warriors won against the Phoenix Suns, with a final score of 115-86. He finished the game with a total of thirteen rebounds, sixteen assists, and a final score of fourteen points.

Steph achieved success once again when he made another triple-double on February 28, 2014. His statistics included eleven rebounds, eleven assists, and a final score of twenty-seven points. In this game, the Warriors defeated the New York Knicks, with a final score of 126-103.

On April 11, 2014, the Warriors won against the Los Angeles Lakers and Steph once again recorded a triple-double. His stats included ten rebounds, twelve assists, and a total score of thirty points. The final score was 112-95.

By the end of the season, Steph's statistics included an average of two steals, eight assists, and a score of twenty-four points per game. Once again, Steph helped the Warriors advance to the NBA Playoffs in which the first round involved a series of games against the Los Angeles Clippers.

On April 19, 2014, the Warriors emerged victorious in Game 1 in which the final score against the Clippers was 109-105. This game was led by Klay Thompson who had twenty-two points. He was followed by David Lee with twenty points, and then by Steph with fourteen points. Steph also had three steals and seven assists.

In Game 2, held on April 21, 2014, the Warriors lost but Steph had a fifty-three percent field goal shooting percentage.

On April 24, 2014, the Warriors unfortunately lost by two points, the final score being 98-96. Steph had fifteen assists and a final score of sixteen points in this game.

The Warriors tied the series when they won in Game 4, held on April 27, 2014. Steph had seven assists, seven rebounds, and a score totaling to thirty-three points. The final score was 118-97.

Game 5 was won by the Clippers, but the Warriors were determined to win the sixth game on May 1, 2014. True enough, the Warriors emerged victorious, with the final score being 100-99. In this game, Steph had four rebounds, nine assists, and a final score of twenty-four points.

On May 3, 2014, it was unfortunate that the Warriors lost to the Clippers by five points, the final score being 126-121. In this game, Steph scored a total of thirty-three points. He also had three steals, five rebounds, and nine assists. This loss marked the end of the Warriors' season.

In this season, Steph received significant recognition. He made a total of two-hundred-and-sixty-one 3-point shots for the year. He was recognized for being the NBA player with the most 3-point shots made for two consecutive seasons. The NBA community also recognized his and Klay's efforts for having the most combined 3-point shots in one season. He was also included in the All-NBA Second Team. Evidently, Steph had started to be recognized as a top basketball player. He knew that aside from his coach and teammates, the other notable people who had helped him achieve such a status included Dr. Ferkel and Keke Lyles.

Steph's Opportunity to Play in the All-Star Game in 2014

With all of Steph's achievements, it was expected that he would be chosen to join the 2014 All-Star Game. During a fan voting as to who among the NBA players should be included as Western Conference starters, Kevin Durant was the top choice – the next was Steph Curry. It had been awhile since a Golden State Warriors' had been included in an All-Star Game. The first one was Rick Barry in 1976 and the second one was Latrell Sprewell in 1995 – the next one was Steph Curry.

During the start of the All-Star Game, Steph was not doing well as he only made one successful 3-point shot out of his ten attempts. Unfortunately, he only scored a total of twelve points in this game. When he noticed that he was having a difficult time adjusting on the court, he decided to instead concentrate on setting up plays for his teammates. He made a correct decision in doing this as his eleven successful assists led to the seventy-six combined points of Blake Griffin and Kevin Durant.

Steph's Pre-2014-2015 NBA Season

Prior to the start of the 2014-2015 season, Coach Mark Jackson's contract was unfortunately terminated. The Warriors players expressed their support for Coach Mark, but the Warriors' team executives had already come to an agreement to terminate him due to some issues arising among the coaching staff.

This was a sad event as Coach Mark was able to successfully develop the abilities of the Warriors' players. However, some analysts also said that in spite of what Coach Mark had contributed to the team, he somewhat failed to maximize the skills of his players.

It was on May 14, 2014, when the Warriors executives announced the appointment of Steve Kerr, an ex-NBA player, and commentator on NBA on TNT, as its new head coach. He signed a five-year deal with the Golden State Warriors worth twenty-five million U.S. dollars.

Steve used to be an NBA player himself, having played for the San Antonio Spurs and the Chicago Bulls. Between 2007 and 2010, he was appointed as the General Manager and President of the Phoenix Suns. Prior to his appointment as the new Golden State Warriors coach, he had no coaching experience. However, he was –and will always be – known as one of the best 3-point shooters. While Steph had been vocal about how he admired Mark Jackson as the team's head coach, he was also open about the fact that Steve could be able to help the team improve their offense and, at the same time, be able to help Steph improve his own game.

Before the next NBA season started, the Golden State Warriors picked Leandro Barbosa and Shaun Livingston to join the team as additional guards. This decision further improved the team's roster. In spite of rumors that Klay Thompson would be traded for the Minnesota Timberwolves sharpshooter Kevin Love, the team's final decision was to continue the great tandem of Steph and Klay as the Splash Brothers. Klay then signed a new four-year deal with the team that was worth approximately seventy-million U.S. dollars.

Not getting Kevin Love was actually a tough decision for the Golden State Warriors head office. While they badly wanted Kevin, letting go of Klay and replacing him only meant that the team would need to adjust their entire offensive scheme. They opted instead to allow the Splash Brothers to continue the remarkable tandem that they had started. The Warriors officers made the right choice, and this was evident during the Splash Brothers' performance at the FIBA Basketball World Cup that was held in Spain in 2014.

In that particular FIBA Cup, it was Kyrie Irving of the Cleveland Cavaliers who was awarded the Most Valuable Player award. Nonetheless, nobody could deny the fact that the Splash Brothers remarkably contributed to the achievements of the team. It was teamwork at its finest.

After Team USA won gold at that FIBA Cup, and after the stellar performances of both Steph and Klay, the Splash Brothers became more confident to play for their team.

Despite being sad about the termination of Coach Mark, the Warriors' players were excited to be guided by their new coach. Both the Warriors players and staff knew that Steve's past experience as an NBA player was an advantage to their team as Steve had a first-hand experience of what it takes to win a championship.

With Brandon Payne as Steph's personal trainer, and Keke Lyles as the team's performance director, Steph successfully improved both his strength and his basketball skills prior to the start of the next season. When Steph first entered the NBA, he was considered to be small, weak, and prone to injuries. By the start of the 2014-2015 season, he had well and truly changed that perception.

With the help of Keke and Brandon, Steph focused on enhancing his stability and overall balance. He was not working out to bulk up because doing so would only make him heavier which could aggravate the pressure on his ankles. Instead, he concentrated on workouts that would make him stronger but, at the same time, would maintain his weight.

Steph placed a lot of focus on further enhancing his ball-handling skills. He worked tirelessly with his trainer Brandon on this facet of his game. One of their drills or training methods included Steph having to dribble a tennis ball – yes, a tennis ball – while sitting down. He had to make different dribbling moves using a tennis ball every day for a minimum of one hour.

Brandon also asked him to do drills while facing a wall filled with light bulbs. The bulbs would flash various colors of light from time to time and each color had a meaning. For example, the blue light meant that he had to tap the ball using his off hand while the yellow light meant that he had to do a crossover. He had to do this while his other hand was dribbling a tennis ball. Basically, what Brandon wanted Steph to learn was to skillfully switch between a range of dribbling moves with either hand.

Brandon also instructed Steph to enhance his passing skill by throwing passes while wearing goggles. To make this drill difficult, Brandon made him wear goggles that blocked one of his eyes. Amazingly, Steph could easily do this drill, and so Brandon instructed him to do a more challenging drill. This time, Steph's pair of goggles featured flashing lights that aimed to distract him while making passes.

Steph's Performance During the 2014-2015 Basketball Season

It was in this season when the Golden State Warriors began to experience one victory after another. Their victories paved the way for them to be the leading team in the Pacific Division.

The skills of Andrew Bogut were now being effectively utilized. Andrew was able to create plays that would allow Klay to expedite the offense and free Steph from time to time of the ball-handling tasks. Aside from the improved offensive patterns of the Golden State Warriors, Coach Kerr also improved the team's defensive performance. In the case of Steph, Coach Kerr was able to help him improve his stats in November 2014 to an average of three 3-point shots made, eight assists, five rebounds, and twenty-four points per game. His free throw shooting percentage was also an amazing ninety-three percent while his field goal percentage was fifty percent.

It was amazing that Steph's skills were improving while being guided by Coach Kerr. Coach Kerr would regularly invite Steph to one-on-one free throw shooting matches. They would also have 3-point shooting matches to further enhance the skills of Steph.

The rapport established by Coach Kerr with all the Warriors players, and his efforts to improve the team's capabilities even before the new season began resulted in their strong start during the season. The team also seized their opportunity when several players from different NBA teams seemed to have suffered injuries during the season. This included Manu Ginobili, Tony Parker, and Kawhi Leonard of the San Antonio Spurs, and Kevin Durant and Russell Westbrook of the Oklahoma City Thunder.

From November to December 2014, the Golden State Warriors won sixteen games. It was literally one win after another until they lost to the Memphis Grizzlies in a game held on December 16, 2014.

By January 2015, Steph had already played in almost three-hundred-and-seventy games and had already successfully made one-thousand 3-point shots by January 7.

It was also during this time when Klay scored a total of fifty-two points in a single game. In the third quarter of the game, he scored a total of thirty-seven points. He broke the record of NBA players Carmelo Anthony and George Gervin who both experienced scoring thirty-three points in the third period of a game. This achievement was made by Klay on January 23, 2015 when the Golden State Warriors played against the Sacramento Kings. The Warriors won with a final score of 126-101.

In that particular game against the Kings, Steph exhibited his unselfishness by taking a backseat and allowing Klay to score for the team. Steph only scored a total of ten points, but he also had eleven assists, the majority of which were to Klay.

The tremendous teamwork of the Splash Brothers was an indication that there was genuinely no rivalry or selfishness between them.

On February 4, 2015, however, it was Steph's turn to lead the game between the Golden State Warriors and the Dallas Mavericks, in which the Warriors won with a final score of 128-114. Steph scored a total of fifty-one points, making sixteen shots out of his twenty-six field goal attempts, and ten 3-point shots out of his sixteen attempts.

After Klay scored a total of fifty-two points in a previous game and Steph scored a total of fifty-one points in this game, the Warriors became the very first NBA team in history to have two players that scored more than fifty points in one season. This victory paved the way for the Warriors to lead the league with a record of 39-8. This came as a surprise among the other NBA teams as the Warriors emerged as the number one team in the West. During this time, their counterpart in the East was the Atlanta Hawks.

Steph's and the Warriors' NBA Achievements in 2015

The Golden State Warriors successfully secured the Pacific Division title in March 2015 when they defeated the Portland Trail Blazers. They were also recognized for having the highest number of road wins in one season. Moreover, they were also acknowledged for getting more than sixty wins in one season – in fact, they had a total of sixty-seven wins in the season.

Of course, aside from the achievements of Steph and the entire Warriors team, Coach Steve Kerr was also individually recognized for breaking the record as the team's coach with the highest number of wins. What made it even more remarkable was the fact that it all happened in his first season.

The Golden State Warriors not only broke the records of other teams and players, but they also broke their own records! Steph and Klay had previously made a combined total of four-hundred-and-eighty-four 3-point shots, but they broke that record with five-hundred-and-twenty-five 3-pointers made in 2015.

This season, Steph finished in fourth place for the highest number of steals, sixth place for assists, and sixth place in scoring. His free throw shooting percentage was ninety-one percent, which was recognized as the best in the 2015 season. Between March 2015 and April 2015, Steph made a total of fifty-two straight foul shots without a miss.

Steph's Unstoppable Achievements

As the Golden State Warriors led the league in the 2015 NBA season, the name "Stephen Curry" evidently emerged when the topic of conversation was about the Most Valuable Player. Everyone knew how improved a player he was, not only in terms of his basketball skills but also his unselfish contributions to his team. However, Steph was not the only NBA player who seemed to standout in the 2015 season. There was also Anthony Davis of the New Orleans Pelicans and Russell Westbrook of the Oklahoma City Thunder.

This season, Anthony placed number one in terms of shot blocks, number eight in rebounding, and number four in the total number of points. Meanwhile, Russell had a total of eleven triple-doubles. However, both Anthony and Russell seemed to experience some struggles as their teammates suffered injuries during the season.

Aside from Anthony and Russell, Steph's competition also included James Harden of the Houston Rockets and LeBron James of the Cleveland Cavaliers. Harden's accomplishments included having thirty-three thirty-point games, ten forty-point games, and two fifty-point games in one season. Meanwhile, LeBron had always been one of the most dominant NBA players.

When the voting for the Most Valuable Player was finally completed, LeBron James emerged as the third placer. James Harden was the second placer and Stephen Curry bagged the Most Valuable Player award.

The last time the Golden State Warriors had a player that earned the Most Valuable Player award was in 1960 – it was

Wilt Chamberlain. Now, after several decades, the award was once again received by a Warriors player. Aside from being the Most Valuable Player, Steph was also recognized for helping his team record sixty-five victories.

In Steph's acceptance speech, he highlighted several factors that helped him achieve success. He first emphasized having faith in our Creator more than anything else. Then, he emphasized on having faith in himself. His own belief that he could always improve himself was what helped him achieve the Most Valuable Player award.

Steph also emphasized the importance of passion in achieving success. He said that faith was nothing if one does not have passion for what he is doing.

He also emphasized the significance of grit in achieving success. He had overwhelming courage and drive to improve every single day.

Lastly, Steph emphasized the importance of will to achieve success. It can be recalled that in spite of being a star player in grade school and in high school, he was never offered a college scholarship by any major conference school. He was not even offered a scholarship by his father's alma mater. He also was not liked by the NBA coaches and scouts because he was short and lanky.

It seemed like his dream of becoming a professional basketball player was unlikely. Nonetheless, his strong will prevented him from giving up. He may not have had any choice but to enroll in an unknown college, but he knew that he would do everything to make his dream come true.

This very first Most Valuable Player award and all the other awards he got prior to that were, in fact, only the start of his many other achievements in the future.

Chapter 5: Becoming A Champion

2014 - 2015

After their impressive performance during the 2014-2015 regular season, the Golden State Warriors were the favorites to win the championship.

The Warriors continued their strong play, and powered through the playoffs, until they emerged as the Western Conference Champions, and advanced to the finals.

On June 4, 2015, the Golden State Warriors were ready to play their first game of the 2015 NBA Finals against the Cleveland Cavaliers. The Cavaliers were a strong team led by LeBron James, who was supported by the team's point guard, Kyrie Irving. Many had debated over who the better point guard was – Kyrie or Steph.

Early in first game, things weren't looking good for the Warriors. The Cavaliers held a lead at the end of the first quarter. The Warriors realized that they had to go on the offensive and came back with a vengeance. In the second quarter they fought back, but the Cavaliers were still ahead at the half with a score of 51 points to the Warriors' 48.

In the fourth quarter, Steph was blocked by none other than Kyrie Irving. The scores were tied, and the game went into overtime. Fortunately, the Warriors rallied and scored 10 points in overtime to secure the win.

The second game was very similar to the first. The score was once again tied in the fourth quarter. This time, however, the victory went to the Cavaliers. Despite the absence of Kyrie Irving, LeBron James managed to will his way to victory. The series was now tied at one game apiece.

Steph scored 27 points in the third game, which was the top score made by anyone from the Warriors. The game was a close one, but the Cavaliers managed to defeat the Warriors 96-91, leaving the Warriors down in the series 2-1.

In game four, Steph combined with Andre Iguodala to score 22 points each. In every single quarter, the Warriors were in the lead. Though the Cavaliers put up a good fight, they were no match for the Warriors. The Warriors comfortably secured the win, and tied the series once again!

Steph stepped up again in game 5. He dropped 37 points in the game, and in the fourth quarter, he was a key factor in securing the win. The Warriors were now just one win away from championship glory, but if the Cavaliers won Game 6, the scores would be tied, and a seventh game would be called for. Steph was determined to end the finals in Game 6 and win his first NBA Championship.

While the Warriors were in the lead for the first two quarters of the sixth game, the Cavaliers had put up a great, and it wasn't clear which team would win. There was no room for the Warriors to get comfortable. Once again, Steph and Andre stepped up and scored the highest points for the Warriors, with 25 points each.

The Warriors managed to hold on to their lead and win game six with a final score of 105-97. The 2015 NBA Finals were over. The Golden State Warriors had defeated the Cavaliers in six games and were crowned the NBA champions!

2015 - 2016

After reaching championship glory, Steph had signed a contract with the Warriors to keep him part of the team until the 2016-2017 season.

2016 was an exciting year for the Golden State Warriors and for Steph Curry, but ultimately it ended in a disappointment. The Golden State Warriors had made it to the 2016 NBA Playoffs, with a record of 73 wins and 9 losses for the season.

Once again, the Warriors flew through the playoffs to once again face the Cleveland Cavaliers in the NBA championship series.

The Golden State Warriors were up against perhaps the most formidable player in the NBA, LeBron James. They also had one of Steph's contemporaries – another stellar point guard, Kyrie Irving. The teams went head-to-head, and although

Golden State had managed to lead in the first two games, Cleveland caught up in Game 3. Golden State bounced back and won Game 4 to snag a 3-1 lead. It looked as if another championship was almost certain for the Warriors.

Cleveland then won Games 5 and 6 to tie the series at 3 games apiece. Then, the final game arrived. Steph had been one of the highest scorers for the series and was determined to win the Championship.

The pressure could not have been more immense. Whichever team won Game 7 would become the 2016 NBA Champions. The game was close, but Curry struggled.

With a few minutes remaining, Golden State were down by four points. With the time ticking down, the ball was with Steph Curry. He shot a 3-pointer to try and keep the hope of winning the game alive, but he missed. The Cavaliers held on to their lead and became the first team to ever come back from a 3-1 deficit to win an NBA Championship series. It was a bitter way for Steph and the Warriors to end the season.

2016 - 2017

In 2017, the Warriors were determined to make up for their loss in the previous year's championship series. In this year, they also added superstar Kevin Durant to their team during the offseason, and were now more formidable than ever!

This year, the Golden State Warriors were once again to compete in the NBA Playoffs. Just like the previous two years, they sped through the playoffs to make it to the NBA championship series.

As fate would have it, the rivalry between the Golden State Warriors and the Cleveland Cavaliers was to continue once again as the teams faced each other in the NBA Championship for a third year in a row.

Each team had secured one Championship, and this year would determine who the most dominant team really was. The Cleveland Cavaliers were hell-bent on maintaining their Championship status and securing another title. The Golden State Warriors had only one focus in mind: to redeem themselves by defeating the Cleveland Cavaliers and reclaiming the Championship.

The first game of the series occurred on the first of June. The game was played at the Oracle Arena in Oakland, California. While their home arena brought the Warriors comfort, it also brought them the added pressure. They had faced a humiliating defeat the previous year, and now all eyes were on them.

The game was a close one. At halftime, the Golden State Warriors were up, but only by a small margin. The third quarter was dominated by the Golden State Warriors, who went on a 13-0 run. Steph scored twenty-eight points in this game, but the top scorer was Kevin Durant, who managed to score thirty-eight points. Their combined efforts were enough to secure a game one victory, with a final score of 113-91.

The second game followed a similar script. The Golden State Warriors dominated the Cleveland Cavaliers again, winning 132-113 and moving to a 2-0 lead. This also marked their fourteenth consecutive postseason win.

Game three was held in Cleveland, and while the Warriors held the lead at half time, the Cavaliers were fierce, and they were not going to accept defeat easily. Late in the game, the Cavaliers were leading with 113 points to the Warriors' 107.

There were less than three minutes left in the game, but the Warriors didn't quit. It would seem unlikely if it was not witnessed by thousands in the stadium and millions at home, but the Warriors managed to score 11 points in the short span of time left in the game.

Kevin Durant led the scoring, followed by Klay Thompson, followed by Steph Curry. The splash brother duo of Steph and Klay had now become a tremendous trio of Steph, Kevin, and Klay. With a final score of 118 points, they had secured their third win of the 2017 NBA Championship series. This was their fifteenth post-season win, a record which still stands.

Two days later on the ninth of June, it was time for game four. If the Warriors could win this game, the series would be over, and they'd once again be crowned NBA Champions. Once again, the game was held at the Quicken Loans Arena in Cleveland.

The Cavaliers were determined to not be swept, and the very first quarter they scored an impressive 49 points, which set a record for the most points earned in any quarter of a finals game.

The lead became insurmountable as LeBron James and Kyrie Irving both contributed incredible performances. They ended the Warriors' winning streak with a final score of 137-116.

Game five saw the teams head back to the Oracle Arena in Oakland. The series was sat at 3-1, and a victory in this game for the Warriors would mark the end of another NBA season.

The first quarter was nerve-wracking. Each time the Golden State Warriors scored, the Cleveland Cavaliers answered back. Any time a team was in the lead, the lead was short-lived as the opposing team would outscore them by a small margin.

The second quarter remained close, but ultimately ended with the Warriors in the lead.

The Cavaliers rallied back in the third quarter, and at the start of the fourth quarter it was anyone's guess as to who would win the game.

Steph Curry and Kevin Durant stepped up in the fourth quarter, with Steph sending assists to Kevin allowing him to score whenever possible. However, with each basket that the Warriors scored, it seemed as if the Cavaliers had several baskets to match. Steph knew that this would be a close game just as the seventh game of the previous NBA Final was.

There were less than 50 seconds left on the clock, and the ball was in Steph's hands. He had failed to score in the final moments of game seven in the year prior, but that didn't seem to affect his confidence at all. Steph shot the ball from 3, looking to secure the victory for his team. The ball went in, and Steph Curry brought the Warriors' score up to 129 points, way ahead of the Cavaliers' 115. The Cavaliers managed to score another five points, but it was too late. Nine points ahead, the Golden State Warriors became the 2017 NBA Champions.

2017 - 2018

The 2017-2018 season went in a similar fashion as the prior three years for Stephen Curry and the Golden State Warriors. They seemed to effortlessly advance to the finals and were once again the favorites to win the NBA Championship.

This year, the Cavaliers were without their superstar point guard Kyrie Irving, who had requested a trade to the Boston Celtics at the end of the prior season. This only made it all the more likely that the Warriors would win if they were to face the Cavaliers in the finals for a fourth time.

The Warriors blazed through the playoffs, and once again had made it to the NBA finals. They had a dominant team, with

Steph Curry, Klay Thompson, Kevin Durant, and Draymond Green all being named as NBA All-Stars during the regular season.

Despite the lack of Kyrie Irving, the Cavaliers had once again made the NBA finals.

In the previous year, the Warriors had won the series 4 games to 1. This time, they were keen to assert their dominance as the best team in the NBA by sweeping the Cavaliers in 4 straight games – and that's exactly what they did.

Despite LeBron's best efforts, he was no match for the skills and unselfish play of the Golden State Warriors.

The Warriors won game one with a final score of 124-14.

Game two also went the Warriors' way, with a final score of 122-103.

Game three was the closest of the series, but the Cavaliers still couldn't do enough to win. The Warriors secured a 3-0 lead with a final score of 110-102.

Steph Curry and the Warriors needed just one more victory to secure the Championship for the second year in a row. They continued to dominate in this game and ended the series with an emphatic 108-85 victory!

This marked their third NBA championship in four years, and Steph Curry's third NBA championship also!

At the time of writing, the Warriors have continued to dominate through the 2018-2019 season and are once again the favorite to win the Championship for a third consecutive year.

It's hard to know just how many years the Warriors will dominate for, and how many Championship rings Stephen Curry will be able to secure by the time his career is over. One thing is for sure though, he has changed the game of basketball with his incredible shooting ability, and has already created a lasting legacy in basketball history!

Conclusion

Thanks again for taking the time to read this book!

You should now have a good understanding of Stephen Curry, and his incredible life and basketball career!

If you enjoyed this book, please take the time to leave me a review on Amazon. I appreciate your honest feedback, and it really helps me to continue producing high quality books.

CPSIA information can be obtained
at www.ICGtesting.com
Printed in the USA
LVHW080959140322
713397LV00015B/205